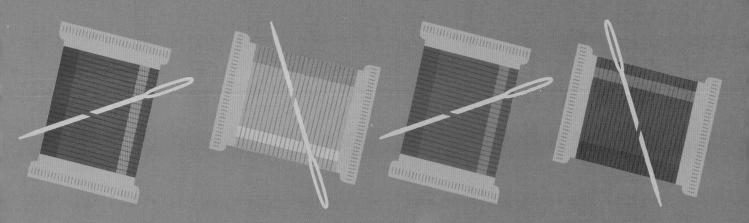

Hobby Time!

SEWING

JANE MARLAND

PowerKiDS
press

CONTENTS

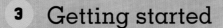

GETTING STARTED

Sewing is a fun and exciting craft activity, and an easy one to master—all it involves is joining pieces of fabric together with a needle and thread! This book will introduce you to the essential skills you'll need to get into sewing by hand.

There are 11 projects to try in this book, with clear instructions to help you get the techniques right. Each one will teach you new skills to help you master sewing. Practice each new stitch a few times first, then jump into an exciting project!

When you're ready to take your sewing a step further, you'll find some great ideas for more challenging activities at the back of the book.

The great thing about sewing is that you can make your creations exactly the way you want them. You're in charge—so let your creativity run wild! Once you've started, you'll be itching to stitch!

SEWING KIT ESSENTIALS

All you need to get started with sewing is some fabric and a simple sewing kit. This can all be found in craft supply stores.

FABRIC

COTTON This fabric is soft but feels nice and crisp. This makes it easy to mark with chalk, cut out, and sew.

FELT A soft fabric that doesn't **fray** and is easy to cut into shapes.

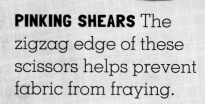

PINKING SHEARS The zigzag edge of these scissors helps prevent fabric from fraying.

EMBROIDERY THREAD Used for decorative stitching and working with felt, embroidery thread comes in "skeins" made of six strands. Use one or two strands when working with delicate fabrics, and three or four strands when working with felt.

Don't use your dressmaking scissors to cut paper as this could blunt them.

SCISSORS Use dressmaking scissors with longer blades for cutting out fabric and smaller ones for snipping threads.

NEEDLES Buy a pack of needles with different sized holes (called "eyes") so you can choose the best one for the project.

PINS Pins are handy for keeping your fabric in place while you sew.

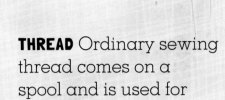

CHALK PENCIL Use this to mark lines on fabric before cutting it. The chalk marks can be wiped off when you've finished the project.

THREAD Ordinary sewing thread comes on a spool and is used for sewing cotton fabric.

TAPE MEASURE Use this to measure your fabric accurately.

RIBBON OR WEBBING Good for making handles or ties.

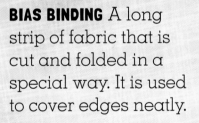

STUFFING A lightweight material used for projects requiring shape.

BIAS BINDING A long strip of fabric that is cut and folded in a special way. It is used to cover edges neatly.

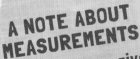

A NOTE ABOUT MEASUREMENTS Measurements are given in U.S. form with metric in parentheses. The metric conversion is rounded to make it easier to measure.

CUSHION INSERT To fill cushion covers.

BUTTONS Add them to your projects for a pop of color!

STITCHES AND TECHNIQUES

All of the stitches in this book are simple to do. Take your time and don't worry if your stitches are not all the same size—it will add to the handmade charm of your project!

1. THREADING A NEEDLE Cut the end of the thread so it has a blunt edge. Gently push the thread through the eye of the needle, then take hold of it from the other side and pull through.

2. STARTING YOUR WORK Make a knot in one end of your thread. When you start to sew, bring your needle through the fabric so that the knot lies on the **wrong side**.

3. FINISHING YOUR WORK Take the needle through to the wrong side of the fabric. Make a small stitch, but don't pull the thread tight; just leave a loop. Bring the needle back through the loop to form a knot. Repeat once more, then cut the thread close to the knot.

Fabric usually has a right side (the side you want to show off) and a wrong side (the side you want to hide from view).

RUNNING STITCH

This stitch is to lightly hold pieces of fabric together. Bring the needle through the fabric, then make a stitch by putting the needle through the fabric a short distance away. Bring your needle back up, the same distance as the first stitch. Continue weaving your needle in and out of the fabric to create a dashed line of even stitches.

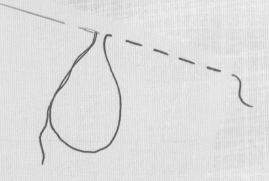

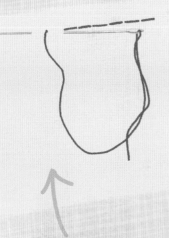

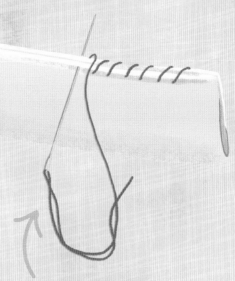

BACKSTITCH

The backstitch is used to hold pieces of fabric together securely. Make two running stitches, then bring the needle back to the end of the first stitch. Bring it out again one stitch ahead. Continue.

OVERSTITCH

This stitch sews two edges together. Bring the needle out to one side of the fabric. Push it back through both edges of the fabric, then out again a bit further along the seam. Continue until the gap is closed.

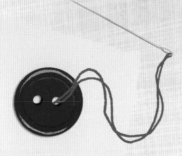

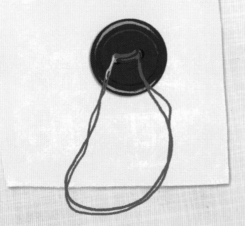

SEWING ON A BUTTON

Thread your needle and knot your thread. Place the button on your fabric and bring your needle up from the wrong side through one of the button holes.

Push the needle back through the other hole. Pull the thread tight, then go back through the two holes a few times to secure.

Finish with a backstitch and knot on the wrong side.

LAVENDER BAG

Lavender bags are fun to make and are a great way to practice your running stitch.

STEP 1

Cut out two 5-inch (12 cm) squares of fabric and **trim** the edges with pinking shears.

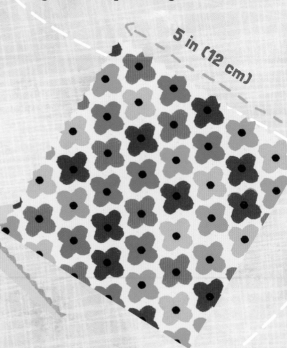

5 in (12 cm)

YOU WILL NEED

· Needle
· Pins
· Scissors
· Pinking shears
· Thread

· Tape measure
· Teaspoon
· Cotton fabric
· Lavender

STEP 2

Pin the two squares together with the right sides facing out.

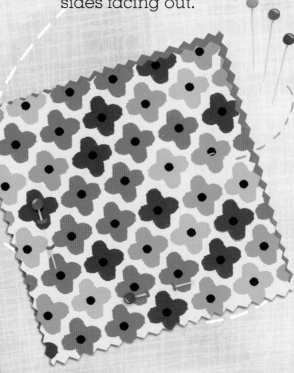

For every project in this book, remember to start and finish your stitches securely.

STEP 4

Keeping your needle out of the way, fill your little sewn pocket with lavender.

STEP 3

Starting as close to the edge as you can, sew a small running stitch along three sides of your square. Remove the pins, but not your needle and thread.

STEP 5

Sew across the gap with a running stitch as you did before.

SHAPE UP

Try cutting your fabric pieces into different shapes and sizes!

FUNKY FELT FLOWER

Choose a thread color that contrasts with your felt colors to really show off your running stitch!

YOU WILL NEED

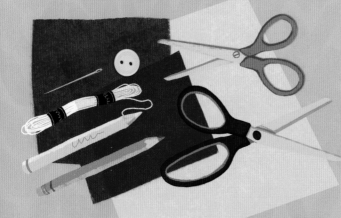

- Needle
- Paper scissors & sewing scissors
- Pencil
- Chalk pencil
- Tracing paper
- Embroidery thread
- Scraps of felt in two different colors

STEP 1

Trace the two flower **templates** from page 32 onto tracing paper and cut them out.

STEP 2

Place the larger flower template onto your first scrap of felt and draw around it with your chalk pencil. Cut out the large flower, then repeat the process with the smaller flower template and the second piece of felt.

STEP 3

Sew a running stitch round the edge of each of the two flower shapes.

Use three or four strands of embroidery thread when working with felt!

STEP 4

Lay the small flower on top of the large flower and place your button on top. Sew the button on to the middle of the flowers through both layers of felt.

Don't forget to wipe the chalk marks off your fabric!

FLOWER POWER

Try making a flower with three layers instead of two!

BUNTING

Bunting always brightens up a room, so why not make some for your bedroom?

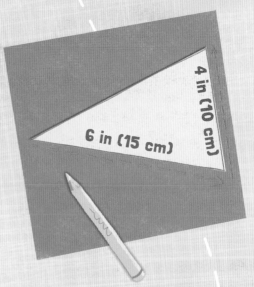

STEP 1

Make a triangle template from card stock. The short side should be 4 inches (10 cm) and the two longer sides 6 inches (15 cm) each. Using your template draw six triangles onto your first fabric six times, then draw another six triangles on the second fabric.

YOU WILL NEED

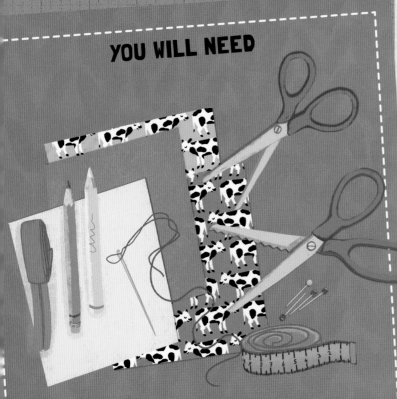

- Needle and thread
- Pins
- Scissors
- Pinking shears
- Pencil
- Chalk pencil
- Tape measure
- Thin card stock
- Cotton fabric (at least two different colors or patterns)
- 3 foot (1 m) pack of bias binding

STEP 2

Cut out your triangles. Use normal scissors for the short side, but cut the long sides with pinking shears to prevent them from fraying.

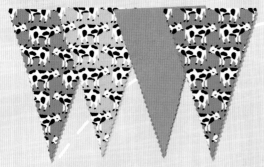

STEP 3

With the right sides facing out, match up two triangles of the same fabric to make each flag. Lay your flags out in the order you'd like.

STEP 4

Unfold the bias binding and mark 6 inches (15 cm) from one end with a pin. Place a flag at this point, then fold the binding down so that the top edge is covered. Pin in place.

STEP 5

Pin the flags 1 inch (2 cm) apart, checking that both sides of the flag are sandwiched between the binding. Pin the tail edges together too.

STEP 6

Sew all the way along the bias binding with a running stitch, removing your pins as you get to them. Make sure you sew the flags and bias binding together.

COLOR CONTRAST

Try using bias binding in a different color or pattern from the fabric to create a contrast.

HANGING DECORATION

Use a cookie cutter to make a hanging decoration!

STEP 1

Draw around your cookie cutter onto your felt twice, and cut out both pieces.

STEP 2

Cut out two eyes from your black felt using a hole punch. Sew the eyes to one of the felt shapes with one or two small backstitches. Sew two buttons to the middle of the same shape.

YOU WILL NEED

- Needle
- Pins
- Scissors
- Black thread
- Embroidery thread
- Chalk pencil
- Hole punch
- Gingerbread man cookie cutter
- Stuffing
- Brown felt
- Small scrap of black felt
- Two buttons
- 7-inch (18 cm) length of ribbon

STEP 3

Draw a smile on your gingerbread man's face and sew over it using a backstitch.

STEP 4

Fold your ribbon in half and sandwich it between the two felt shapes, about ½ inch (1 cm) from the top. Pin the ribbon and the two shapes together.

STEP 5

Sew a running stitch all the way around the shape. Pause about three-quarters of the way around. Put stuffing inside the shape, poking it into the nooks and crannies. Be careful not to strain the stitches! Continue sewing the gap closed with a running stitch.

DOUBLE UP

Sew a smaller layer of felt to the top layer with an overcast stitch before sewing the decoration together.

PURR-FECT PHONE HOLDER

Personalize a phone holder with a fun felt cat.

STEP 1

Put your phone on the felt and mark ½ inch (1 cm) past each side of the phone's width with chalk. Fold the felt over your phone and mark ½ inch (1 cm) past the top of the phone with chalk. Cut out the felt following your chalk guides.

YOU WILL NEED

- Needle
- Pins
- Sewing scissors
- Paper scissors
- Pencil
- Chalk pencil
- Embroidery thread
- Tape measure
- Hole punch
- Felt for phone case
- Phone
- Tracing paper
- Felt scraps for cat's head, eyes and nose

STEP 2

Trace the cat template from page 32 onto tracing paper and cut it out. Draw around it on to your cat's head felt and cut out. Cut two small black circles for eyes using a hole punch, and a pink triangle for the nose.

STEP 3

Sew the eyes and nose in place with a few small stitches. Draw some whiskers and a mouth and sew over this line with black thread using backstitch.

STEP 4

Fold the phone case felt in half and carefully pin the cat to the top layer of felt only. Unfold your felt.

STEP 5

Using an overstitch, stitch the cat to the felt.

STEP 6

Fold the felt in half and pin the two halves together. Sew down each side using an overstitch, then remove the pins.

OINK

Use the same template to make a pig! Use pink felt and sew on a button for its snout.

SHIRT CUSHION

Work your sewing magic on an old shirt and transform it into a stylish cushion cover!

YOU WILL NEED

- Needle
- Pins
- Scissors
- Thread
- Chalk pencil
- Tape measure
- Iron
- An old shirt with buttons on the front
- A 14-inch × 14-inch (35 cm × 35 cm) cushion insert

STEP 1

Button the shirt up and draw a 13-inch (32 cm) line across the front. Place pins at either end of the line, going through both sides of the shirt. Make sure the buttons are in the middle of the line.

STEP 2

Draw a 13-inch (32 cm) line down from each end of the horizontal line and join to form a square. Add pins at each corner, through both sides of the shirt.

STEP 3

Cut this square out through both layers of the shirt and remove the pins.

STEP 4

Place the two squares together with wrong sides facing out (with buttons on the inside) and pin.

STEP 6

Undo the buttons and turn your cushion cover right side out. Poke the corners out gently and iron the cushion cover (ask an adult to help you). Insert your cushion pad and do the buttons up.

STEP 5

Starting as close to the edge as you can, sew around all four sides with a backstitch.

PICK POCKETS

Choose a shirt with pockets — then your cushion will have pockets too!

ALPHABET KEY RING

These super cute key rings make great gifts!

YOU WILL NEED

- Needle
- Pins
- Sewing scissors and paper scissors
- Chalk pencil
- Embroidery thread
- Paper
- Small pieces of felt in two colors
- Stuffing
- Mug or cup
- 3-inch (8 cm) length of ribbon
- Key ring attachment

STEP 1

Draw around the mug on to the first color of felt twice, and cut out two pieces.

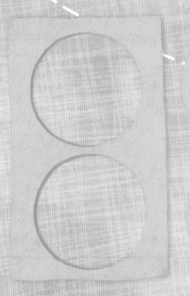

STEP 2

Print out or draw a capital letter to fit in the middle of these circles and cut out. Draw around the letter onto the other color of felt and cut out.

For letters with holes in the middle (such as A, B and D), sew the inside section first, then sew around the outside.

STEP 3

Pin the letter to the middle of one of the felt circles and sew in place with a running stitch.

STEP 4

Fold your ribbon in half and sandwich it between the two felt circles, very close to the top. Pin the ribbon, then pin the circles together.

STEP 5

Sew a running stitch all the way around the circle. Pause about three-quarters of the way round.

STEP 6

Put stuffing inside the circles, then sew the gap closed with a running stitch. Attach a key ring to your ribbon loop.

SPOTS AND STRIPES

Use a fun printed fabric for your letter for a different look.

PENCIL ROLL

This project will make a roll to fit eight pens or pencils.

YOU WILL NEED

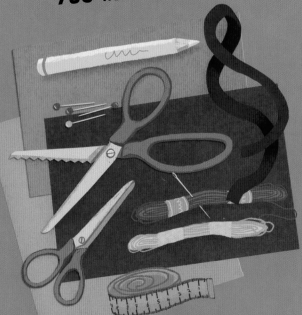

- Needle
- Pins
- Scissors
- Pinking shears
- Chalk pencil
- Embroidery thread
- Tape measure

- 1 piece of cotton fabric measuring 9 inches × 10 inches (23 cm × 25 cm)
- 2 pieces of felt measuring 8 inches × 10 inches (20 cm × 25 cm)
- 24-inch (60 cm) piece of ribbon

STEP 1

Trim the edges of the felt and fabric pieces with pinking shears. Fold the cotton fabric in half lengthways with the fold at the top—this will be your pocket. On the right side of the fabric, draw a vertical line 2 inches (5 cm) from the left edge. Repeat for the righthand edge.

2 in (5 cm)

STEP 2

Draw another vertical line 1 inch (2 cm) from the line you drew on the left. Repeat four more times—you should have seven lines in total.

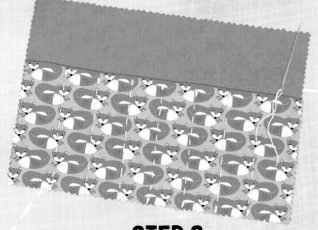

STEP 4

Place the felt piece with the pocket on top of the second felt piece. Fold the ribbon in half and tuck the folded end in between the two pieces of felt, just above the top of the pocket. Pin everything together.

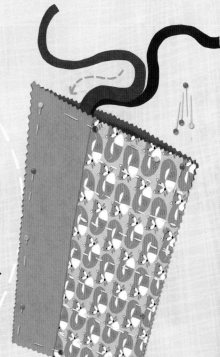

STEP 3

Place the pocket on top of the first felt piece, lining up the bottom edges, and pin it in place. Using backstitch, sew down each stitching line, through both layers of cotton and the felt.

STEP 5

Starting close to the edge, sew a running stitch around all four sides, making sure you stitch through all the layers. Remove all the pins. Now it's time to add some pencils!

BRILLIANT BORDER

Add some ribbon to the edges when you sew the layers together to create a pretty border.

EASY TOTE BAG

Choose a bright, contrasting color for the handles to make your tote bag really stand out!

YOU WILL NEED

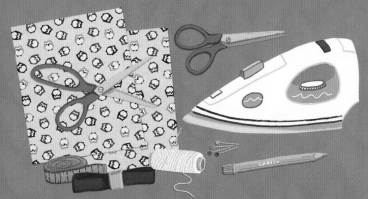

- Needle & thread
- Pins
- Scissors
- Pinking shears
- Chalk pencil
- Tape measure
- Iron

- 2 pieces of cotton fabric measuring 12 inches × 14-inch-wide (30 cm × 36 cm)
- 2 pieces of 1-inch-wide (2 cm) webbing or ribbon, measuring 20 inches (50 cm) each

STEP 1

Trim the edges of your fabric with pinking shears. On the right side of your fabric, measure 3 inches (8 cm) from the top-left corner along the top edge and mark with your chalk pencil. Do the same on the top-right corner, then repeat for your second piece of fabric.

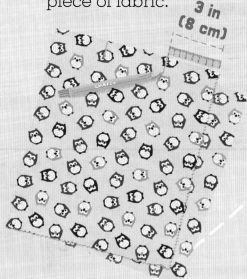

3 in (8 cm)

STEP 2

Fold ½ inch (1 cm) of webbing under itself and pin to the first mark. Then pin the other end of the webbing to the second mark, again with ½ inch (1 cm) folded under. Repeat with the other piece of fabric and webbing.

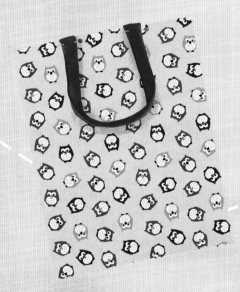

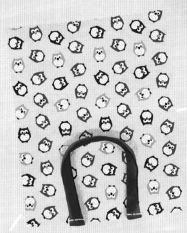

STEP 4

Turn the fabric pieces over to their wrong sides. Fold the top edge over by 1 inch (2 cm) and pin. Iron this fold into place to give a crisp edge. (Ask an adult for help.)

STEP 3

Sew both handles down with a backstitch and remove the pins.

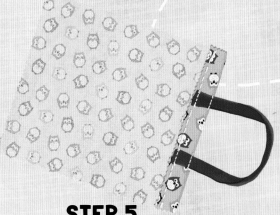

STEP 6

Put the two pieces of fabric on top of each other with wrong sides facing out and pin. Starting close to the edge, sew along all three sides of the bag using a backstitch. Turn your bag the right way out.

STEP 5

Secure the handles even more with a backstitch near the top of the fabric fold. Then stitch along the bottom of the fold with a small running stitch.

LITTLE AND LARGE

You can make this bag smaller or larger. A tiny tote would make a gorgeous gift bag!

DRAWSTRING BAG

This useful drawstring bag is perfect for holding all your bits and pieces.

YOU WILL NEED

- Needle
- Pins
- Scissors
- Pinking shears
- Thread
- Tape measure
- Iron
- Safety pin
- Polka-dotted fabric measuring 11 inches × 28 inches (28 cm × 72 cm)
- Ribbon measuring 34 inches (85 cm)

STEP 1

Trim the edges of your fabric with pinking shears.

STEP 2

On the wrong side of your fabric, measure 2 inches (5 cm) down from the top edge at each side and mark. Join the two marks with a line. Do the same on the bottom edge.

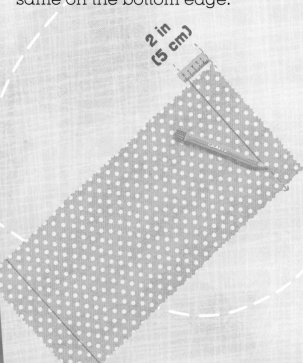

2 in (5 cm)

STEP 4

Fold the edges over at the stitch line and iron so they lie closed (ask an adult to help).

STEP 3

Fold the fabric in half lengthways so the wrong sides face out and pin. Starting at the chalk line, sew down each side using a backstitch. Remove the pins.

STEP 7

Secure a safety pin to the end of the ribbon. Feed it through one tunnel, across the gap and through the other tunnel. Remove the safety pin. Make both ends of your ribbon the same length, then tie the ends together.

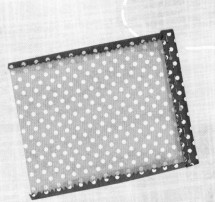

STEP 5

Fold (or iron) down the top of the bag until the zigzag edge lines up with the chalk line. Pin. Repeat for the other side.

STEP 6

Stitch along the bottom of the fold with a running stitch. Repeat on the other side of the bag. Remove the pins.

PICTURE IT

Make the bag in a plain fabric and sew patterned fabric to the front before sewing the sides together.

JUGGLING BALL

Juggling balls are fun to sew and are a really unusual gift idea!

YOU WILL NEED

- Needle
- Pins
- Sewing scissors
- Paper scissors
- Pencil
- Chalk pencil
- Embroidery thread
- Teaspoon
- Tracing paper
- Felt scraps in four different colors
- 3 ounces (80 g) dried lentils or rice, for filling

STEP 1

Trace the juggling ball template from the back of the book and cut out. Pin this shape to a scrap of felt and cut around it. Repeat for the other felt scraps.

STEP 2

Lightly draw a cross with a chalk pencil on one side of each of your four felt shapes. The side with the cross on will be the wrong side.

STEP 3

Lay one shape on top of another with the wrong sides facing out and pin. Sew along one curved edge using a small overcast stitch. Remove the pins.

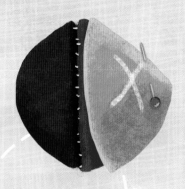

STEP 4

Unfold what you've just sewn so that you have the right sides facing you. Place the third shape on top of the second shape with right sides facing. Pin, stitch, and unpin as before, then repeat with the final shape. You should now have an inside-out juggling ball, all stitched together apart from one gap.

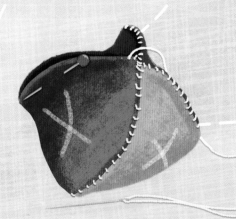

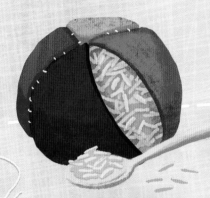

STEP 5

Pin the right sides of the two unlinked shapes together. All the sides you can see should have crosses on them to show that they're the wrong sides.

STEP 6

Partly stitch the last shapes together, then unpin and turn the shape inside out. Using a teaspoon, fill the ball with lentils or rice until it's nice and plump.

STEP 7

Pin the edges together and sew closed using an overstitch. Unpin.

TRIPLE IT

Now that you've successfully made one juggling ball, why not make two more for a complete set?

NEXT STEPS

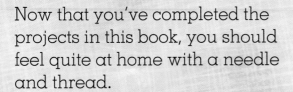

Now that you've completed the projects in this book, you should feel quite at home with a needle and thread.

CUSTOMIZE YOUR CLOTHES

Expand your hand-sewing skills by having a go at **customizing**. Cut out fabric or felt shapes and stitch them to your clothes for an individual look.

BEGINNER SEWING CLASSES

If you are feeling confident and would like to take your sewing a step further, you may be ready to start sewing on a machine.

Look out for classes in your area, which are often run by local schools, councils, or community centers. A beginner sewing class should teach you how to set up and thread a sewing machine, as well as how to sew in a straight line.

All of the projects from this book that include straight lines of running stitch or backstitch can also be completed on a sewing machine.

JOIN A SEWING CLUB

Sewing clubs are often held in specialist sewing schools or craft cafés, and are a great way to meet other sewing fans. They may also offer introductory sewing lessons or classes.

SIMPLE GARMENT SEWING

If you enjoy using a sewing machine, then why not have a go at making your own clothes? A good first **garment** to make is a pair of pajama bottoms—lots of places offer this kind of class, as pajamas are easy to fit and sew!

GLOSSARY

CUSTOMIZE To change something to your own personal taste.

FRAY When a cut edge of fabric unravels or wears away.

GARMENT A piece of clothing.

RIGHT SIDE The side of the fabric that you want to be seen.

TEMPLATE Paper or card stock used as a guide to make copies of shapes.

TRACE To copy a pattern or drawing using thin paper (tracing paper) that you can see through.

TRIM To cut off the edges of fabric with scissors.

WRONG SIDE The side of the fabric that you don't want to be seen.

USEFUL WEBSITES

PowerKids Press has developed an online list of websites related to the subject of this book. This site is updated regularly. Please use this link to access the list:

www.powerkidslinks.com/ht/sew

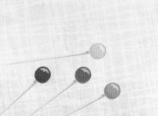

INDEX

Published in 2018 by **The Rosen Publishing Group, Inc.**
29 East 21st Street, New York, NY 10010

Cataloging-in-Publication Data
Names: Marland, Jane.
Title: Sewing / Jane Marland.
Description: New York : PowerKids Press, 2018. | Series: Hobby time! | Includes index.
Identifiers: ISBN 9781499434347 (pbk.) | ISBN 9781499434286 (library bound) | ISBN 9781499434163 (6 pack)
Subjects: LCSH: Sewing--Juvenile literature.
Classification: LCC TT712.M37 2018 | DDC 646.2--dc23

Editor: Liza Miller
Designer: Simon Daley
Illustration: Esther van den Berg
Photography: Simon Pask Photography

Manufactured in China
CPSIA Compliance Information: Batch #BS17PK: For Further Information contact Rosen Publishing, New York, New York at 1-800-237-9932.